The Challenges Facing Management

The Challenges Facing Management

DON G. MITCHELL

FORMER PRESIDENT

GENERAL TELEPHONE AND ELECTRONICS CORPORATION

THE CHARLES C. MOSKOWITZ LECTURES

SCHOOL OF COMMERCE, ACCOUNTS, AND FINANCE

NEW YORK UNIVERSITY

THE CHARLES C. MOSKOWITZ LECTURES

THE CHARLES C. MOSKOWITZ LECTURES were established through the generosity of a distinguished alumnus of the School of Commerce, Mr. Charles C. Moskowitz of the Class of 1914, who retired after many years as Vice President-Treasurer and Director of Loew's, Inc.

Mr. Moskowitz's aim in establishing the lectures was to contribute to the understanding of the function of business and its related disciplines in society, by providing a public forum for the dissemination of enlightened business theories and practices.

The School of Commerce, Accounts, and Finance and New York University are deeply grateful to Mr. Moskowitz for his continued interest in, and contribution to, the educational and public-service program of his alma mater.

CONTENTS

FOREWORD by Dean John H. Prime   vii

ASSURING A DYNAMIC ORGANIZATION   3

GETTING THE JOB DONE   19
THROUGH DECENTRALIZED MANAGEMENT

RESEARCH AND DEVELOPMENT—   37
THE KEY TO THE FUTURE

CASE HISTORY I   63

CASE HISTORY II   69

THE SECOND SERIES OF THE CHARLES C. MOSKOWITZ LECTURES was delivered by Mr. Don G. Mitchell, former President of General Telephone and Electronics Corporation, in November 1961. The recipient of seven honorary degrees from American colleges and universities, he serves as Chairman of the Board of Directors of the American Management Association and as a trustee of the Committee for Economic Development.

Mr. Mitchell is nationally recognized as one of industry's leading management authorities. In these three lectures he presents a penetrating analysis of the challenges that face the management of a dynamic organization. He views decentralization of operating units as a vital aspect of managerial development and as an extremely important factor in developing sound employee and plant-community relations. At the same time, he regards vertical integration as one of the most effective means of achieving and maintaining high-quality products at the lowest possible costs. His discussion of these problems should prove to be of inestimable value to those who bear the responsibility of managing American industry.

John H. Prime, DEAN
SCHOOL OF COMMERCE, ACCOUNTS, AND FINANCE
NEW YORK UNIVERSITY   MARCH 1963

The Challenges Facing Management

1.

ASSURING A DYNAMIC ORGANIZATION

AMERICAN INDUSTRY is in the third year of a new decade that will present more opportunities and more challenges than ever before in this country's history. For years, American industry has effectively set the pace for the rest of the world, but now the situation has changed. American industry is at the crossroads today: We have the choice of participating in the growth and development of the world market and continuing to be the leading factor in the world economy, or we can miss this opportunity and gradually be outdistanced by our competitors throughout the world. However, this is much more than a new situation for American businessmen—it is also a new situation for the entire country. The great advances in communications and in the ability of the people of the world to maintain effective contact with one another, together with the rapid advances in all branches of technology, have combined to eliminate effectively the obstacles of time and distance which in years past inhibited world trade. The trade horizons of every country have greatly broadened, and businessmen throughout the world are seeing opportunities for increased trade that they never saw before.

This economic revolution throughout the world is far more than a trend that involves only large industries. It profoundly affects every industry and every business. In its relative way, the small business in a small town is just as deeply involved as the country's major corporations. Every one of us, big and small, is faced with a whole new set of opportunities and challenges.

Let me be more specific about these opportunities and challenges, so that we can relate them more directly to our individual businesses. I will list them first, and then examine each of them more closely.

1] We must place greatly increased emphasis on *research and development*—or, to put it another way, on *innovation and invention*. Aside from constantly improving our goods and services and producing them at competitive costs, we have the even greater challenge of developing entirely new products and services, new ways of making them, and new ways of getting them to customers next door or on the other side of the world.

2] We must assure far *greater automation and mechanization* of both our manufacturing and administrative processes. Only through greater automation can we attain the higher volume, lower costs, greater flexibility, and higher efficiency that we will need to compete in the world markets.

3] *We must streamline our management.* We must do a better job of organizing and instill in our management people that dynamic point of view that makes things happen, that encourages teamwork, that encourages the delegation and acceptance of responsibility.

4] *We must adapt our operations more effectively to our existing and potential markets.* In other words, if a market exists overseas, and the best way to take advantage of that opportunity and to meet competition is to establish manufacturing facilities overseas, we must be flexible enough to do just that. Worldwide markets require a worldwide viewpoint, and to acquire this we must change some ideas and practices that we have had for years.

5] Finally, *we must revitalize the American point of view.* We must recapture the drive, the enthusiasm, the ideals that produced this fantastic economy of ours. This means *taking risks.* It means entrepreneurship and business-pioneering. It means exercising our ingenuity and moving into new areas and in new directions.

Research and Development

When we talk about the future of our economy, we customarily talk in terms of the gross national product and its annual rate of growth of 3 or 3½ percent. Now this, of course, affords an excellent measure, especially in comparing past and present performance. But there is an intangible that we should also factor in, and that is the steady progress in technology—the refining and improving of our products, the developing of new principles, new designs, new materials, new efficiencies. In other words, economic growth comes not only from gradually increased consumption of traditional products and services, but also from the consumption of entirely new products. That is where the big potentials are.

When you bear in mind that it takes from 7 to 10 years on the average to translate the findings of research into a new product, and that from 50 to 75 percent of the products of many large companies today are completely or radically different from the products of 15 years ago, you can see why the emphasis on research has increased so drastically in recent years. Back in 1941, the total spent throughout the economy on research was less than $1 billion annually. Today it is more than $14 billion annually, of which industrial research and development represent at least $10.5 billion, and the figure is climbing all the time.

Let the conservative who wonders whether all this expenditure is worthwhile remember first the vital importance of research in national defense, and let him also remember that some entirely new major industries have evolved since the war—electronics, petrochemicals and plastics, for example. Moreover, such major industries as communications, aviation, and electrical manufacturing have gone through enormous change.

But let me cite something even more specific that proves the value of research: studies by the National Science Foundation show that research pays off at the rate of 100 to 200 percent a year. This means that $100 spent on research will bring back a total of from $2,500 to $5,000 over a 25-year period, depending, of course, on the industry and the company.

Research for many years was identified almost entirely

with the highly technical industries, but the picture has changed, and we now find an almost universal interest in research throughout industry—not only in manufacturing but in transportation, agriculture, mining, and most recently in distribution. But this interest, great as it is, must be accelerated and strengthened, and we must find ways of at least doubling our research spending over the next few years. The challenge is as simple as this: What we do in our laboratories today and tomorrow and next year, and the skill and speed with which we apply those research findings, will determine the position the United States will hold in the critical latter years of this new decade. The seeds for the new products that we will need in seven or eight or ten years to answer our new and expanding needs must be planted *now*.

Automation and Mechanization

It is extremely important to bear in mind that I do not mean increased production volume alone, but also lower costs, greater flexibility, and higher efficiencies. Making more of a given product is only part of the story, and in certain market situations it may even be the last thing we want to do. But getting lower and lower costs is something else again, because a great potential danger for American industry is finding itself priced out of the world market. The challenge can be boiled down to this: The manufacturing side of industry must generate obsolescence in our production processes and develop more efficient and less costly processes just as fast as it can. If it doesn't, foreign prices will put us right over a barrel.

Greater manufacturing efficiencies, backed up by effective research and development, constitute a formidable answer to competition from abroad.

Automation requires very close analysis, because its long-term benefits can be obscured by short-term dislocations. The demagogue likes to conjure up the vision of great numbers of our working force being thrown out of work, but what he ignores consciously or unknowingly is an unassailable fact: machines remove drudgery; they don't remove jobs. Certainly, there are short-term dislocations, and avoiding or resolving those situations requires every bit of skill and planning that management can apply. But the end result of automation in the manufacturing plant is the elimination of obsolete jobs, and the creation of new, better, and higher-paying jobs.

When one gets right down to it, the plants and equipment we have in industry today could never begin to do the work required of them as our country grows and its demands for new and improved products increase. Aside from at least maintaining our present rate of automation, we will have to do an even bigger job. When one thinks in terms of our exploding population, which will reach 200 million by 1970, the steadily rising living standards of those people, and a gross national product moving toward $750 billion by 1970, one can see why American industry will have to gear its thinking and its performance to an entirely new set of demands. In fact, it has been estimated that automation will, in effect, have to fill 20 million job vacancies over the next 20 years, because there will not be enough skilled people in the working force to produce the goods and services we will need and demand in the future.

The opportunities to use automation to keep costs in line and to realize many other benefits are not restricted by any means to the manufacturing side of the business. There is not a businessman in the country who does not wish that he could do something about the mountain of paperwork that confronts him day after day—most of it just so much past history about which he cannot do anything anyway. The American businessman must do something about speeding up the entire process of administration. Although the administrative side of the business has made great improvements in efficiency in recent years, the typical manager receives reports, surveys, and statements, all of which represent thousands of manhours of tedious and costly work, most of them of relatively limited value because the situations being reported are beyond correction, and the best that can be done is to apply those safeguards which one feels will prevent their happening again, or which will at least minimize them. The challenge is not only to do something about the *volume* of paperwork we plow through every day, but also to get the *right* information—the information we really do need—and get it in time to do something about it. To put it another way, we must have a wider variety of usable information faster than ever before. Some excellent progress has been made in solving this problem through *administrative automation,* but we have only scratched the surface.

Let me cite some figures. The cost of clerical employment in industry today is estimated at more than

$30 billion, and it is steadily climbing. Some 15 years ago, there were about 5 million clerical employees, or 11 for each 100 manufacturing employees. The number of clerical employees is more than twice that today: the ratio is more than 16 for each 100 manufacturing employees, and the number is growing. I realize full well that the administrative problems of running a business are greater than they were 15 years ago, but the main point is that business has become so complex in its administrative operations that better, faster, and less expensive ways of doing administrative work must be found. Automation is the only answer. What this really means, of course, is electronic data-processing—the gathering, processing, summarizing, and reporting of a wide variety of information relating to accounting, payroll, production, costs, inventories, shipments, and so on. This is not the place to go into the relative merits of various types of electronic data-processing systems and how the job can be done best. Suffice to say, however, that taking the drudgery out of paperwork and making the job more efficient and less costly are other aspects of keeping our costs competitive so that American business can get its share of the world markets.

The Necessity for Streamlining Our Management

This means that a priceless ingredient of success is having the kind of management team that sets the right goals and attains them with the minimum of blood, sweat, and tears. This is not by any means a problem confined to the large organization, because a small company can become just as disorganized and just as ineffective in its own way as the largest corporations in the country.

The biggest danger in any organization is the failure to identify the problem and do something about it. A dynamic organization will seek out problems, it will identify them, it will decide upon the best solutions, and it will assign the obtaining of that solution to somebody and hold him responsible. In these days of growing competition from abroad in our markets here at home and growing opportunities to trade in new markets abroad, the need not only for an action-centered organization but for an organization that acts on the right situations at the right time is more critical than ever.

I do not know of a better way to assure the proper environment for a dynamic organization than to have a policy of decentralized management. Let me define decentralization: *It is the delegation of authority and accountability so that every decision made in a company is made at the lowest level where that decision can be intelligently made.* A great many people say that decentralization is the physical dispersion of properties, but they are wrong. It happens to be easier to operate a decentralized organization in a series of small, physically dispersed plants than in a large, centralized plant because it is much more difficult for the top management to walk in and try to run things, rather than leave the division and department managers alone. When the plant is 100 miles way, it is easier for top management to stay in the headquarters office and let the manager run the plant himself.

When you put a manager on his own and give him full authority to run his operation—subject, of course, to the policies and controls any organization needs to have if it is not to become a group of airtight compartments doing just as they please—you are taking a major step toward getting things done the way they should be done. That manager *has* to be dynamic and action-centered if he wants to do the job you have given him. There is also a bonus here: the morale effect does not stop with the manager; it permeates to all of the people in his organization because they know from his attitude that he is the boss, and not some distant headquarters 100 miles away. We have found that gives them a great sense of local pride, and you can sense it the moment you walk in that plant door.

The divisions of the writer's company that have more fully and effectively accepted the policy of true decentralization—that is, the ones that do not follow either of the two extremes of dumping everything in top management's lap or running too far afield with the ball—are the quickest to sense and act upon the opportunities available to them. In a number of cases, this has given us a priceless head start that we otherwise never would have had.

Overseas Expansion

The challenge is to establish manufacturing and service facilities abroad in order to participate in the expansion of markets there. It seems to me that there has been a great tendency to regard the rebirth and growth of the economies of the free world purely from the standpoint of competition. Certainly, they represent new competition, but that should not concern us if we step up our research and our automation. But the broader and more important aspect is the opportunity to expand and develop our operations abroad so that we can serve those expanding economies and participate in their development.

Western Europe, for example, is far more than the nations of the Common Market and the Free Trade Association, all of whom are justifiably seeking to promote trade among themselves and with the rest of the free world. Far more importantly, Western Europe, with a total output of goods and services roughly equal to 60 percent of the United States total, represents enormous opportunities for American industry, just as the United States has provided opportunities in the past for European industry. Here is our greatest opportunity and our greatest challenge: the economy of Western Europe, which has a greater potential than Russia and the Iron Curtain countries. To me that is an enormously comforting thought, because these competitors are our allies, and we are on the same side in our competition for the world markets.

These opportunities overseas have not passed unnoticed. During the past eight or nine years, American industry has doubled its investment in operations abroad, and the net result has been that total sales of products made by United States plants overseas are rising faster than exports from the States. At least 3,000 American companies have invested some $50 billion in foreign manufacturing and marketing, and nearly $30 billion alone is invested in operations in which American companies have a 25 percent or greater interest. That $30 billion, incidentally, is more than double the amount of 10 years ago.

Because of the magnitude of this investment, there is every probability that sales from overseas operations will at least double in the next 10 years. Frankly, that estimate is probably too conservative, and the increase could well be threefold, particularly in Western Europe. It is certain that the increase will be substantial, because private investment from the United States is climbing steadily in Western Europe, and today it is up around $5 billion, which is three times the total of 10 years ago. And, based upon the trend that has been established, a figure of $6 to $7 billion could be reached in the next three or four years. Again that could well be conservative, because American manufacturers are currently putting nearly 50 percent of their overseas capital expenditures into Europe.

In looking at the trade potential in Western Europe, we cannot, of course, disregard the trade barriers that are inherent in a common market. But I do believe that most of the dislocations that do occur will be relatively short term, and there will be no great permanent detriment to outside countries. The important point to bear in mind is that we in the United States are in an economic situation entirely different from any that we have ever encountered before. It will require plenty of give and plenty of take, but this has always been the case, especially since the end of World War II. The ball game will be the same; the only difference will be that we will be playing more games on the other team's home grounds. Provided we stay competitive, through the steps that I discussed earlier, we have only to look forward to an unprecedented era of growth and development, both here at home and in the new markets abroad.

The Necessity for Revitalizing the American Point of View

We must renew the enthusiasm and the pioneering spirit that symbolize this country of ours. It seems to me that there is an unusual amount of ultraconservative or negative thinking these days, and too great a tendency to concentrate on the "sure thing," to avoid reasonable risk. The new college graduate who in his first job interview asks about the pension plan epitomizes that point of view. Certainly I am not advocating that management should jump headlong into a situation without studying it and developing sound courses of action, but a business organization should be in business to *do* something—to expand its services, to provide broader opportunities for its owners, its employees, and its customers—and not to rest on its laurels. This is the space age, and the American businessman is being launched into situations he has never encountered before. In these days when space vehicles and satellites are more and more commonplace, we should not forget that none of these amazing things would have happened if our country's scientists had not looked for and *found* entirely new ways of doing things. They took a positive viewpoint, made up their minds that the job could be done, and then proceeded to do it.

That is the challenge confronting all of us in business today. We must concentrate far more on finding entirely new ways of doing things, we must be prepared to discard traditions and the "sure thing" if we know down deep within us that there are better ways to do it. And if we do not know of better ways to do things, we simply are not looking hard enough.

There is not a roadblock that anyone could devise that could be an obstacle to American industry, provided that American businessmen apply their *ideas, imagination,* and *drive,* with every bit of *vigor* and *enthusiasm* they can muster.

If this is done, every dream and every goal that the individual company has set for itself will be realized.

2.

GETTING THE JOB DONE THROUGH

DECENTRALIZED MANAGEMENT

THE COMPLEXITY OF MODERN SOCIETY certainly encourages the impression that twentieth-century living is a gigantic merry-go-round, and that life consists of being put on the colorful horses for a certain length of time and being pulled off without warning when your time runs out. Modern living may be downright confusing at times, but there are certain fundamentals that are predominant, and they are contained in that all-embracing phrase: *"the satisfaction of human needs."* Every facet of modern society is, in some way, engaged in "satisfying human needs"—whether it be industry, education, government, unions, the arts and sciences, or anything else.

As a spokesman for industry, let me point out that industry is certainly aware of its vital importance in modern society, but that it certainly does not regard itself as *the* focal point. This is important to bear in mind, because the trends in industry today appear to be so far-reaching that at times they may seem to overshadow other areas. Such is not the case. There is only one focal point, and that is the *individual*. Regardless of his role in society, the individual is the center around which all other forces rotate. It is only when someone begins to think that the *individual* should begin rotating around some *force* that trouble occurs. To put it another way, it is only as long as the rights and the integrity of the individual are safeguarded that society progresses. When the individual is submerged, society begins to retrogress. There have been many examples of that in history, and today a similar process is taking place behind the Iron Curtain.

When you seek to analyze industry, and appraise its performance, you sooner or later come to the realization that you are evaluating *people*. You will start out with financial information and production information and you will be amazed at the size and scope of industrial operations, but sooner or later you will find yourself studying what this person did, or what that person meant by a certain policy decision, or how Joe is doing in a certain job. What you are really talking about when you talk about industry is "people"—not capital expenditures, or inventories, or raw materials, but "people." Large or small as it may be, any industrial organization is not some vague mass known as "the Company." It is a group of fifty, or five hundred, or fifty thousand human beings engaged in a common effort, with varying degrees of success, to provide telephone service, produce a space satellite, make an airplane, or television sets, or shoes, or bicycles, or countless other things.

Organizations are live, they are vocal, and they function twenty-four hours a day, seven days a week. You cannot turn them on and turn them off. They are a manifestation of action and reaction, of person reacting to person, of cause and effect, of influence and counter-influence.

The organization, then, is not some inanimate thing that drives individuals. It is an instrument *for* individuals, created by them and intended to serve them. To the extent that people are submerged or restricted so that others may have inordinate privileges, the organization is undesirable because some individuals are acting to the detriment of others. However, if the organization is a means of fostering group action for the common good, provides benefits for the individual and helps him meet his legitimate needs, then the organization is as it should be.

This brings us to a consideration of the trends of the past three quarters of a century, a period that witnessed the development of today's tremendous industrial economy. The vast economic benefits which have come over the years have been described many times and are well known to each of you. Yes, they have created the highest standard of living the world has ever known, but what has been the overall effect on the individual—the person who helps to produce those benefits? Can you obtain steadily increased material benefits without steadily decreasing individuality and destroying personal relationships? Do you increase economic productivity and weaken human relations?

Let me answer those questions first, and then tell why I think as I do. I do not feel that there is anything inherent in our industrial system which necessarily leads to a loss of individual identity. Loss of identity does not arise from the *magnitude* of modern industry. An individual working in a ten-man office may have far less identity than someone who is part of a 3,000-man working force in an industrial plant. The problem of identity revolves around the question of *attitude*. Certainly no one reading this feels that he has lost any identity by being one of some 180 million people in the United States. If he does, would he feel that he would gain identity by being one of 25 people in an isolated Eskimo camp in the Arctic circle?

This problem of recognition is a quite natural outgrowth of the tremendous size of industry, since that very size tends to merge individuals into large groups. And there is an understandable tendency, in the pressure of modern business, to think of the group rather than the people who comprise it.

But that does not excuse the tendency—it merely explains how it comes to be. One of our manufacturing managers hit the nail right on the head the other day when he said, "When we talk about changing this or that production schedule, let's not forget that we are talking about *people*—we're talking about telling *people* to make more or less of something, and we're shifting *people* from one job to another."

The overriding significance of individual attitudes is reflected in the fact that, no matter how different their respective fields of endeavor may be, all industrial corporations seem to fall into one of two different categories: 1] those that take things as they come, and   2] those that create opportunities and make things happen. The overall problem seems to be the degree in which a given company's employees sense the opportunities to do a better job, to take advantage of new opportunities, and to set the pace for the competition.

There is little or no reward in simply preserving the status quo in any business—even if that were possible, and I am sure that it is not. No company can stand still in an expanding economy; it either moves ahead or slips back. The real payoff comes with leadership. You may never attain first position, but that is not the really important point. *Striving* to attain leadership is 99 percent of the battle. However, striving for leadership, or to be one of the leaders, presupposes that you have the management strength not only to see the opportunities but to take advantage of them. It is a point of view that is wonderful to have and takes plenty of hard work to achieve.

From the standpoint of any top management, the challenge is to make sure that you have so organized and so equipped and so trained your management that they are operating with a point of view and in a climate that breeds success. No matter how brilliantly conceived, no management concept can succeed unless the individual managers down the line have the will and the determination to make that concept succeed.

I do not know of a more effective way to foster and to encourage that determination than through *decentralized management*—the delegation of appropriate authority and accountability to the managers of autonomous units or "profit centers." In other words, the job is done at the level where it can best be done, and decisions are made at the lowest possible level in the organization where those decisions can be intelligently made.

Let me repeat a portion of that statement: The job is done at the level where it can *best be done*—not at the next lowest level nor the next higest level, but at the very lowest level where the best job can be done.

Moreover, it is extremely important that decentralization of management not be confused with geographic dispersion of facilities. It so happens that decentralization of management works more effectively when plants are dispersed into relatively small units, but I also know of cases where a relatively large concentration of facilities can be effectively operated as a group of decentralized operations.

Now, let me go back some 20 years and tell you precisely how the many advantages of decentralization first became apparent to Sylvania Electric Products, which is one of the manufacturing subsidiaries of General Telephone and Electronics.

During World War ɪɪ, our large plants in Emporium, Pennsylvania, were producing electronic tubes—tremendous quantities of them for the proximity fuse program, which was regarded as one of industry's great technical achievements during the war. Production was, of course, many times the prewar rate, and our employees came from many surrounding communities, some of them a considerable distance away. Everything proceeded smoothly until an unusually severe snow storm hit that mountainous area, and the highways became impassable.

A large number of the employees couldn't reach the plant.

We decided to solve that problem right then and there. We made the fundamental decision to take the work to the employees. Feeder plants were established in several communities. When the war ended, the natural move would have been to return to prewar methods and again concentrate our activities in Emporium. But we decided not only to maintain these so-called "satellite" or "feeder" plants, but to make them independent operations. That was the beginning of the trend toward decentralization at Sylvania, a trend that has resulted not only in many increased production efficiencies, but has strengthened the identity of the individual employee.

Now let us delve more deeply into the very real psychological effects of decentralization. When you appoint the manager of a decentralized operation, you tell him, "This is *your* plant. *You* decide what to do and when to do it. We've set the ground rules, the broad policies, and controls, but it's up to you to figure out how to operate under them."

As you can well appreciate, this presents a very stimulating challenge to that manager. Knowing that he has the responsibility for the success of that local operation, and that he will not be doing simply what someone else tells him to do, the manager has a sense of pride which is almost as strong as it would be if he personally owned every square inch of that plant.

Furthermore, that attitude permeates the entire organization. Everyone in that plant, from the receptionist at the front door to the shipping clerk at the rear, knows that the local manager, and not some main office hundreds of miles away, is running things. They see that what they do has a direct effect on what the manager does, and that they, as well as he, are *individuals* who have a job to do.

In some companies, just the reverse of that happens. The plant manager has absolutely no independence of thought or action. He lacks any responsibility and authority, and the employees sense it immediately, with the result that they attribute everything that does or does not happen to some vague group in some far-off place. You hear such complaints as, "I wish the home office would make up its mind," and you hear it from everyone, including the manager. There isn't much individuality in that version of "absentee ownership." The individual is a cog, and that is about all.

The exact opposite is the case in the decentralized plant, and you can sense it the moment you enter. When you walk through the plant, you can see by the conversation just what the attitude is. The first names, the joking about yesterday's bowling score, the asking about the son who is in the service—not simply *acting* interested because the book says you should, but rather because you *are* interested—those are the symptoms of a healthy situation.

What are the effects outside the plant? This team spirit, with its mutual respect and understanding, is evident throughout the community. The situation that existed several years ago in one of our company's plant communities is a case in point. The plant manager was a member of the town council. Do you know who the chairman of the council was? One of the foremen in the plant. From eight to five, that manager and that foreman had one relationship. After five, the situation was exactly reversed. That never could have happened unless those two men had wanted it to be that way.

A decentralized plant, operated as an integral part of a community, seems to breed a certain point of view—an awareness of community responsibilities and a desire to do something about them. Whether it is the fund-raising campaign for a new church, the Community Chest, or some other worthy cause, the philosophy that is all so evident stems from the basic fact that each of the persons involved views the project as part of his *individual* responsibility. Just as he identifies himself with the success of that local plant, so does he see that his participation in community affairs is vital.

Let me look at decentralization from another aspect. The only way you can get the best out of a manager and let him at the same time satisfy his desire to be a manager is to let him *manage*. I am sure that sounds like a very obvious point—a sort of corporate truism. However, there are many, many instances where the manager is poised and ready to manage and spends the greater portion of time seeing the responsibility taken away from him by the next man up the line.

Anyone who denies that the greatest temptation in business is to make decisions for the manager next down the line is not being very realistic. If you came up through the marketing organization, as I did, the easiest thing in the world to do is to stroll into the marketing vice president's office and make a few decisions—and the same holds true whether you came from manufacturing, engineering, finance, or anything else. Responsibility and authority go hand in hand; they are inseparable. You cannot hold a man responsible unless you let him make the decisions, and if he would rather you make the decisions, the obvious course is to discourage him from doing so, to put it mildly—or take him out of that manager's spot.

Every so often you observe a managerial technique in industry which is best described as the "leave 'em out in left field" school of management. It works at its best when you hear that a manager has made a bad decision— perhaps even a *very* bad decision. He knows it and you know it, and a lot of other people know it. That is a turning point in his career, and perhaps in yours. You can pull the rug out from under him, and leave him out in left field, or you can back him up, even though you know he is wrong. If you do the first, you have destroyed his usefulness and have lost a good manager. But if you do the latter, you will have gone a long way toward minimizing future wrong decisions on his part, and you will have strengthened immeasurably his contributions to the management team.

The other day I was discussing decentralization with a visitor who was particularly impressed by the high efficiency of decentralized plants. Did the employees work harder, or what? The answer to that question is a very simple one. A decentralized plant is more efficient because everyone in the plant *wants* it to be efficient. They don't work any harder, but they do work more effectively. In other words, a more efficient plant *is* more efficient because there is a higher degree of pride in the job. A less efficient employee may work just as hard as a more efficient one, but he doesn't do his work as well because he hasn't the desire to learn to do it better.

It is a question of that all-important word *"attitude,"* and assuring the right attitude is one of the prime responsibilities of top management.

Now for the inevitable word of caution. Decentralization offers many benefits, but it also contains some pitfalls. The challenge to top management is to prevent the various decentralized, highly autonomous units from becoming airtight compartments, each of them operating on its individual wave length without regard to the effects of its actions upon other segments of the company.

Decentralization requires clearly defined and clearly understood *overall policies* established by top management. It requires *ground rules*. It requires *controls*. This requires constant and effective communication all along the line, from top to bottom, and unless this is achieved, the result is a tangled mess of separate operations, each of them doing just about as it pleases. This is not decentralization. This is dismemberment.

Lest I give the impression that decentralization can be adopted by any industry, provided it has the proper controls, let me hasten to say that decentralization works extremely well in some companies but would be extremely difficult or impossible to apply to others, such as in the manufacturing of locomotives or turbine generators or power shovels—in other words, heavy equipment. On the other hand, our own company is fortunate by the very nature of some of its products, which are broad in variety, and high in value, and small—hundreds of different types of electronic tubes, for example, or lamp bulbs.

We sincerely do not know how far any given company can go in this process of decentralization, but we do know that decentralization has given many companies the product quality and competitive costs so necessary for continued growth. But even more importantly, it is decentralization that has created an employee attitude, a will to do a good job, which has been vital to our progress.

It seems to me that too much emphasis is given these days to a manufacturing technique or process in itself, and not to the point of view, the attitude, that gave birth to that process or technique in the first place. There is a saying that I like to repeat as often as I can find someone to hear it. "No company, no machine, no chemical process ever made anything. Only people make things."

In the final analysis, all companies can develop or purchase just about the same types of machines and the same raw materials. Where, then, is the difference between one company and another? The difference is in the individual. Any company's priceless assets are not its machines but its *people*.

However, these people—these assets—will have little actual value unless they are motivated to do something, to function as a team that has clearly defined goals. Bearing in mind that management is the art of getting things done through people, you must remember that you can't get things done unless you let your people know what your goals are—what you want to accomplish, why you want to accomplish it, how they will benefit from it, and the role they will play in accomplishing it. This is another way of saying that the members of the management team must be able to identify themselves with the company's goals. No chief executive, no top management committee ever reached these goals unaided. Unless the entire management team is aboard, the company will never get where it wants to go.

It goes without saying that all of this presupposes management has set definite goals—not hopes, but *goals*—based upon a sound appraisal of existing trends and the opportunities they seem to provide for further expanding and improving the business. It is a case of setting new and greater goals, and setting sound courses to attain them. Another name for this process is, of course, long-range planning.

Obviously there are definite limitations to long-range planning in a dynamic economy like ours. How can anyone look ahead two or three years, let alone five or six, and predict what will happen with any reasonable degree of certainty? The answer is that you do the best that you can on the basis of the information you have and situations then prevailing, and as new information becomes available and new situations develop, you revise your plans accordingly. The important point, however, is that you are looking as far ahead as you reasonably can and attempting to detect trends and opportunities while they are still in a stage where you can do something about them, rather than dealing purely in current situations over which you have a limited degree of control.

The challenge, in other words, is this: The setting of goals through long-range planning requires a careful blending of practical and imaginative points of view, and the goals must be flexible enough to allow for new situations. Moreover, no plan or goal is any better than the extent to which the goal is communicated to and acted upon by the management team.

There is another important aspect of management communication that deserves comment, and that is the organized and thorough approach to any given problem, idea, or opportunity. There is great emphasis these days on everything coming in a package—witness the package deal, the package TV show, and so on. Similarly, the package deal is a vital aspect of good management communication. I mean the package a good manager presents to top management—the package that describes an idea, tells what is new and different about it, why and how it will help the company, what he thinks should be done about it, and how much it will cost. It may be a new plant, or a new product, or a major problem of some sort, or even buying another company. The point is that it is a package deal. Whether it is an opportunity or a problem—and a problem is simply an opportunity in disguise—the effective manager suggests a solution and tells you why he recommends it. The right kind of manager is the one who presents his problem to you only when he needs some policy clarification, or when he is recommending a change in policy. Furthermore, he always accompanies the problem or recommendation with his solution. Not only that, but this same manager is usually the type who volunteers workable solutions to other people's problems. That kind of man is a wonderful person to have around.

Let me close this chapter by saying that the overall goal of top management, bearing in mind all of the comments I have made, is to be *"action-centered,"* to insist on planned action—not running in circles with "much ado about nothing"—the systematic but imaginative attacking of problems. This requires consistency: the adoption of sound courses of action and sticking to them. There is nothing more demoralizing than the constantly and erratically shifting point of view. Plans should not be inviolate by any means, but they should not be changed simply to change them or to experiment needlessly.

The *positive* view, the searching for new and better ways of doing things, is the thing. *Anybody* can tell you something *won't* work. But the real management man— the dynamic management man—is the man who finds a way.

3.

RESEARCH AND DEVELOPMENT—

THE KEY TO THE FUTURE

IN THE PREVIOUS CHAPTER we analyzed the factors that assure a dynamic organization: the management policies and points of view that take full advantage of the opportunities available to a business organization.

In this chapter we deal with another major challenge—the necessity for placing greatly increased emphasis on research and development, ranging all the way from the unearthing of new basic information through fundamental research to the application of that information to new and improved products and manufacturing processes.

Dramatic, Far-reaching Changes

We are surrounded today by so many startling scientific and technological achievements that we perhaps sometimes lose sight of the fact that the past 50 years have seen more technological progress than all the preceding

37

centuries of man's existence on earth. In fact, we can narrow down this time period even more and say that the past 25 years have seen more technological change than all the preceding years of recorded history. For the first time in the history of man, dramatic, far-reaching changes take place in 10 or 15 years, or in even shorter periods—witness the development of atomic energy and space satellites.

Just think about this for a moment—great changes certainly occurred 75 or 100 years before the twentieth century, but today each one of us can think of at least several outstanding achievements that did not exist 15 or 20 years ago. The lifesaving antibiotics; computing machines; television, both as a technical achievement and as a communications medium; guided missiles; jet engines; the penetrating eye of radar; microwave radio transmission; polio vaccine—I could use the next several pages adding to the list. These are developments of the past few years—of less than a generation—and yet every single one of them has become an integral part of our civilization.

Progress Moving Ahead Almost Vertically

If you were to try to describe graphically the phenomenon of scientific and technological progress, you would find it necessary to set up a chart with "time" running along the horizontal side, and the extent of technological change on the vertical axis. The plotted line would run along the bottom of the chart for century after century; when it reached the nineteenth century it would begin to climb ever so slightly; as it passed the 1900 mark, it would turn upward some more; by 1963, the curve would be shooting ahead almost vertically. Today, progress is moving ahead exponentially; it is progress *times* progress, not progress *plus* progress.

There are several ways you can try to measure what scientific research and development means to our economy. You can measure it in terms of cost, or in terms of the new industries and the new jobs it has created, or the benefits it has brought. There are thousands of new products for industry, commerce, the home, and national defense. Research has conquered diseases that had mystified us for centuries; it has put some 50 to 60 satellites in outer space; it has enabled man to fly an airplane at speeds far greater than sound and to ride in a space capsule around the earth; it has revolutionized our entire agricultural industry with its chemicals and insecticides; it has trebled the number of metals used by industry; and through communications has narrowed the dimensions of the earth to a time interval of a split second—the length of time it takes radio to send your voice around the world.

In many parts of the country where research laboratories are commonplace today, there were open fields as recently as 20 years ago. In the 1920's, there were probably 75 or 100 industrial laboratories at the most, but today there are more than 5,400 industrial research and development laboratories throughout the country. The number of scientists and engineers engaged in research and development exceeds 300,000. I have seen it estimated that more than half of the scientists and engineers in certain industries—the aerospace industry, electrical equipment and communications, fabricated metals, and instruments—are engaged in research and development. It has also been estimated that 85 percent of all physicists, 61 percent of all mathematicians, and 54 percent of all chemists are engaged in research and development.

Industrial Research Costs $10.5 Billion Annually

As I pointed out in my opening chapter, industry's own research and development work costs at least $10.5 billion, or about 2 percent of our gross national product, and that does not include government or university projects.

It has been estimated that about 95 percent of that $10.5 billion for industry as a whole goes into exploiting previous scientific breakthroughs, and that the remainder goes into digging out new knowledge, new fundamental information upon which the breakthroughs of the future will be based. The 95 percent led to the developments I mentioned earlier—the antibiotics, radar, television, and so on—and the remaining 5 percent was directed toward exploring such broad areas as the atom, the forces of the universe, and the various fundamentals of that entire process which we so simply call "life." On the other hand, nearly half of the research work done by university laboratories is basic, which is understandable, of course, in view of the different orientation of these laboratories.

How Research Has "Paid Off"

Without question, scientific research has brought enormous benefits to all of us. Certainly the United States would not have achieved its present gross national product of some $520 billion annually without research having found the means to put to work our natural resources, to satisfy our desire for higher living standards, and to translate our productive skills into tangible products and services. However, is there any way we can measure these immense benefits more tangibly? What does society get back, in dollars and cents, from its investment in research? Why should my company or any other company spend millions of dollars on research and development? As I pointed out in my first chapter, the National Science Foundation recently came up with this amazing answer: Over the past twenty-five years, research expenditures have "paid off" at the rate of from 100 percent to 200 percent each year. For every $100 spent on research and development, the return over a 25-year period has been from $2,500 to $5,000. In relation to our gross national product, the Foundation estimates that research has probably contributed at least 0.5 percent, and more likely 1 percent or more, to the long-term productivity increase of 2.1 percent per year.

In the face of that information, it is abundantly clear that the future of any *company* or any industry or any economy rests on its ability to keep up with its competition by developing new products, new services, and new ways of doing things. In today's competitive situation, there is always some other company right behind you, ready to step in to take your place. No company, no matter how successful it may be today, can decide that what it did last year or the year before will take care of things adequately in the years to come. A motto to keep foremost in mind is that *"Today's research is the key to future success."*

How Long from Laboratory to Market?

You will also recall that I mentioned that the average time lag from the initiation of some new project in the laboratory to the time that a new or substantially improved product appears at the market place is *ten years*. I am not talking about a refinement here and there, or even a major improvement; I mean something basically new, like power-steering, or television, or the heat pump, or electroluminescent lighting, or polyester fibers, or the electric refrigerator. The actual time lag may be seven or eight years in the case of one development, or it may be twelve in the case of another, but the average always seems to work out to about ten.

If I were planning a new research project, however, I would ignore that ten-year span. The important thing to bear in mind is not some average, but rather that *research takes time.* From the standpoint of management, that means you have to adopt what I would like to call a reasonable degree of *impatience* and reduce that time lag to an absolute minimum. Every engineer knows that the completely understandable tendency is to keep that new development in the laboratory until it will work perfectly, while at the other end of the line is the salesman who wants something better than his competition, and wants it *right now,* and not next August.

Well, the answer is somewhere in between. From a practical standpoint, if you wait until a given product will do everything you dreamed it might do, you will *never* introduce it, because if it works perfectly in every respect, it is already obsolete, and you will be in the same position as the man who in 1961 finally developed the perfect "one-hoss shay." So what you end up doing is introducing a product that does something its predecessor could not do, or does the same thing better, and is competitive in price. It is a case of introducing significant and helpful improvements and innovations at the appropriate time from the standpoint of the benefits to the company as a whole, and not one part of it. Each one of these improvements and innovations will add up over the years to a rather startling change over the comparable product of ten years ago.

Research Must Be Continuous

Research and development, and the introduction of the fruits of that research and development, is a continuous, day-after-day, businesslike process. You cannot turn it on or off at the slightest provocation or at the slightest dip in the economic picture. The best analogy I can think of is the hearth furnace—keeping the fires going is vital to a steel mill because if you turn them off, you ruin the furnace and it will cost immeasurable amounts of manhours, money, and lost competitive position before you get the mill running again. So it is with research.

As any member of top management will tell you— especially the director of research and the controller— one of the most difficult problems he encounters is how to determine the extent of the research and development budget. Some companies have a policy that research and development should be a certain fixed percentage of gross sales, and a total is then given the research director to assign to various fields as he deems proper. This percentage, incidentally, may vary from a high of 24 percent of sales in the aerospace industry and 6 percent in the electrical industry to a fraction of a percent in certain other industries that I would rather not name, for obvious reasons. Some companies take a very scientific approach to science and have what is known as a "probability ratio," in which the value of the potential product is multiplied by the probability of successful research, and divided by the cost of research and development.

How Do You Arrive at a Research Budget?

The most practical policy, however, seems to be to compile a list of the various projects that are deemed to be necessary for the company's continued growth and development, putting them in an order of rank that relates them to the company's major lines of business, assigning to each a cost based on an extremely careful analysis of the state of the art, and then arriving at a total, which is then compared with the company's gross sales.

Next comes the really difficult part of the process, and

that is to strike a reasonable and practical relationship between that total cost of the various projects and the company's sales. I don't believe you can or should apply rigid percentages, but you can establish certain benchmarks that experience has proved to be reasonable and practical. This isn't an easy process, for it depends upon such factors as your company's competitive position, the rate of technological change in your major product lines, the confidence you have in your research and development organization, and a reasonable balance between the short-term and long-term outlooks as far as earnings are concerned. Sometimes the practical aspects of a business dictate that certain very important projects must be deferred for a while, but this is a dangerous area for impulsive decisions and must be given all the brainpower the organization has at its command before a final decision is reached.

Research Payoff Comes from Ten Percent of Projects

But the sweat and the toil are worth it, provided you don't expect miracles. I want to make an especially important point of this. Management cannot expect its laboratories to do the impossible; it must resign itself to the fact that a remarkably small percentage of the research projects ever go into production. The payoff is in the small percentage that do. I would hazard a guess that as much as 90 percent of a large company's research ideas don't pan out, but that the remaining 10 percent do and justify the entire cost many times over. Putting research on a crash-program basis may sometimes work in certain types of military programs or in relatively narrow product areas, but you cannot order a man to sit down at a laboratory table and develop a cancer vaccine or a flat-wall television receiver by next April.

Effective and productive research comes from a climate that is hard to identify and hard to define. It is an extremely skillful blend of intellectual freedom and a sense of direction. There have been exceptions, of course, but a laboratory cannot be a never-never land where everyone does as he pleases and takes off on a tangent that may intrigue him. Nor can the laboratory be an intellectual prison where independent thought is inhibited and everything sharply directionalized. The practical answer lies in between, and finding it requires highly developed management skill and leadership.

The foreruners in the field of research today are not the Johnny-come-latelys; they are established industries that realized that their future depended upon the skill, the speed, and the continuity with which they developed new ideas and new ways of doing things. If you were to survey a cross section of these leading companies, you would find that from 50 to 75 percent of their sales today are derived from products that did not exist fifteen years ago. Does a progressive management need any more proof than *that*?

Aside from the development of new and improved products, however, research and development have produced many far-reaching improvements in manufacturing processes and methods. I have primarily in mind the broader use of automatic and semiautomatic machines—in other words, *automation.*

You will recall that I have pointed out that automation has been the key to lower manufacturing costs, greater flexibility in the types and quantities of products, higher and more consistent product quality, and more efficient use of materials and components. I have also pointed out that, from the standpoint of the individual worker, automation has eliminated *obsolete* jobs and has created new, better, higher-paying jobs.

However, let us look at the impact of automation from a broader standpoint, and analyze the changes it has brought across the entire breadth of our economy.

1] Without extensive automation, industry could not even remotely begin to produce the vast volume and variety of goods needed and demanded today by the public, commerce and industry, and the armed forces. In effect, automation has actually met what would otherwise have been a critical shortage of skilled labor.

2] The increased demand for and availability of the products of the highly mechanized industries have brought a great expansion of the basic-materials industries which furnish raw materials and components, such as metals, glass, chemicals, plastics.

3] Greatly increased and improved job opportunities have been created, resulting in better living standards and a great upsurge in education.

4] Thousands upon thousands of small businesses have been formed over the past few years, especially the post-war years, to meet the needs of the mechanized manufacturers. The typical large manufacturing companies, even those by-and-large vertically integrated manufacturers who produce most of their own components and materials, place millions of dollars worth of business with hundreds of thousands of small suppliers and vendors all over the nation.

5] Thousands of communities throughout the country have gained new economic strength, either through the expansion of an existing facility, or the construction of a new plant or laboratory.

6] An enormous new business has sprung up, completely outside the manufacturing side of industry. This is the distribution and service industry, whose distributors, jobbers, and retail dealers constitute the vital link between the manufacturing plant and the market place. This segment of our economy has multiplied manyfold since the war, and will continue to grow very rapidly in the years ahead, for the simple reason that a manufacturing company is no better than the efficiency with which its products are taken to the consumer. Production efficiencies and product quality certainly are vital ingredients of success, but they are meaningless, in the final analysis, unless they are supported by equally effective distribution.

These, then, are the ramifications of automation. It has not put machines to work in one plant or even in one industry; it has expanded existing industries, created entirely new industries, hundreds of thousands of better jobs, and many millions of dollars of additional personal income and buying power.

I hope that the reader will pardon my enthusiasm if I point to the communications industry as an impressive example of the benefits accruing, not only to an industry but to the public it serves, from automation. This industry has had a large-scale revolution in mechanization, and without this revolution the United States could never have achieved the quality, quantity, and versatility of telephone service that it enjoys today. But let me describe this progress in more direct terms. If the central telephone offices and similar facilities were manually operated today, instead of being highly automated, there would not be enough women in the entire working force of this country to do the job. Automation has been the only way that the telephone industry has been able to meet the steadily growing demand for new and broader services.

I would like to cite the General Telephone System as an example. Back in 1955, our telephone companies served some 3,000,000 telephones in various parts of the country; there were about 32,000 employees in the system, and 80 percent of the telephones we served were automatic, i.e., dial-operated. Today, these companies serve 4,700,000 telephones, they have 44,500 employees, and 93 percent of the telephones served by these companies are dial-operated. In other words, automation has not only been the key to better service, but in meeting this need, it has created new job opportunities.

By the same token, we could reach into many other industries and describe the benefits brought by automation. At the same time, however, we cannot ignore the fact that in some industries automation has caused dislocations, and it is no consolation to a man who has lost his job when you point out that technological unemployment is only short-term and that more and better jobs will be created over the long run. All that man knows is that he has lost his job. What can industry do to avoid this situation, or if it does happen, what can industry do to solve the problem?

There is no ready solution to this problem, because even the most efficient of industries will on occasion be confronted with employee-dislocation problems. However, there are a number of long-term and short-term steps that a company can take to minimize the impact of technological unemployment. As I see them, these are the responsibilities of the individual company:

1] *Products and services must be constantly broadened and improved;* the company must keep abreast of scientific and technological change; goods and services must be distributed to the consumers efficiently and at the lowest possible cost, so that the markets are expanded and job opportunities are maintained and strengthened. Some of the most serious problems of technological unemployment and employee displacement have occurred in those industries that have failed to remain competitive, either in terms of costs or in the development of new and improved products and services.

2] *Changes in the technology of manufacturing must be effectively planned and implemented* so that dislocations due to reductions in the jobs available, or in the skills or training required, are kept to an absolute minimum.

3] *All of the employees should be kept fully informed of the various trends and competitive situations prevail-*

ing in the industry so that they can appreciate the problems confronting management, recognize their impact upon the employee, and cooperate in solving them—especially in regard to maintaining high production efficiency.

4] *Employees should be trained or retrained to provide them with new or improved skills* required by current or anticipated employment opportunities for which they may not be presently qualified.

5] If reductions in working force become necessary, *management must schedule these separations* in such a manner that the full benefits are derived from normal attrition in employment and the displaced employees are provided the maximum opportunity to find new employment over a reasonable period of time.

The magnitude of this challenge of adjustment varies, of course, with the industry. The new and rapidly expanding industries that have emerged in recent years, and particularly since the end of World War II, have had virtually the opposite problem. Their problem has been to find enough skilled employees and enough suitable communities in which to locate their facilities. Moreover, this situation has prevailed in spite of the extensive automation which has been undertaken over the years.

The electronics industry is a perfect case in point. From an industry of perhaps $500 million in annual sales just before World War II, electronics is today the fastest growing major industry in this country, with manufacturing sales of $10 billion, and total sales and revenues, including broadcasting, of $15 billion annually.

Without question, this could never have happened

without large-scale automation and mechanization. Without extensive use of automatic and semiautomatic processes, the electronics industry could not even remotely produce the vast volume and variety of goods and services required today by the public, commerce and industry, and the armed services. Automation has been the key to high production volume, competitive costs for the manufacturer and lowest possible cost to the consumer, higher product quality and more uniform product characteristics, and improved product performance. In other words, automation not only met a labor shortage in our industry but gave new skills and new efficiencies to our employees. This is the essence of automation: *The job of the machine is to help the human worker, to take the drudgery out of his work, to free him for more rewarding, more productive, and more stimulating work.*

And so today the electronics-manufacturing operations of our company are part of an industry employing some 1,500,000 persons in manufacturing, distribution, service, and broadcasting, in contrast to total employment of some 70,000 before the war. Here is a clear-cut case where research and development, followed by automation and mechanization to put the fruits of research to work, created an entirely new set of industries—hundreds of thousands of jobs that did not exist, millions of dollars of personal income, and new lifeblood for communities throughout the country.

Thus, the electronics-manufacturing side of General Telephone & Electronics Corporation is basically an example of more jobs created by automation. Our telephone operations reflect a similar situation. The growth and mechanization of telephone service have created *more* job opportunities, not fewer. By way of comparison, the telephone companies of the General System served some 3,000,000 telephones in 1955, with 32,000 employees, and 80 percent of these telephones were dial-operated. These companies serve nearly 5,000,000 telephones today, with 44,500 employees, and more than 93 percent of these telephones are dial-operated. In other words, the entire base has grown, and job opportunities have grown with it (these are not the same types of jobs that existed in 1955; they are *better* jobs, and *better-paying* jobs).

Turning now to the *responsibility of government,* this is twofold. Government has the responsibility to anticipate and to identify those trends that will create chronic unemployment problems in the future, and it has the responsibility to participate in the solution of those problems once they occur. I want to stress that word "participate" because, as I pointed out earlier, this is not the sole responsibility of government; it is the responsibility of industry as well.

First, let us look at the preventative responsibility, the steps government can take to minimize chronic unemployment.

1] At the Federal Government level, the tax laws of this country require a drastic overhauling. This is not a plea for lower taxes simply for the sake of lower taxes, but it is a plea for revamping the entire tax structure so that it *helps* our economy to grow and to prosper, instead of acting as a hindrance.

More specifically, we need new tax provisions to

stimulate plant modernization and expansion, and this can be accomplished by liberalizing depreciation allowances and by permitting faster amortization of new facilities.

We also need a liberalizing of the personal-income-tax rates insofar as dividends and interest are concerned, so that increasing amounts of private capital will be available for investment.

Here again we are talking about accelerating our economic growth by strengthening the ability of industry to spearhead that growth. With a healthy and broadening economic base, those who are among the chronically unemployed will have greater opportunity for new employment, and many who would normally be destined to join the ranks of the chronically unemployed will never find themselves in that predicament.

2] The Federal Government cannot be put in the position of trying to supply a panacea for everybody's ills. Its financial support should be limited to those activities that are logically its responsibility or those situations in which state and local governments cannot do the job. Even the United States Treasury does not have a bottomless money chest, and local communities and state governments should prove their case beyond any reasonable doubt before federal aid is provided. Most importantly, the responsibility for doing the job and the incentive to do it must not be taken away from the local community.

Overriding this entire consideration of governmental responsibility is the necessity for objectively and thoroughly identifying and studying the problems presented by chronic unemployment and developing reasonable and practical plans of action to relieve them. There is a delicate balance here between rushing into a situation before adequate plans are made and the other extreme of procrastinating until the problem is virtually beyond hope. It therefore becomes apparent that the problem of organizing to meet this problem is a critical one. A number of possible solutions have been suggested, including a high-level federal agency that would coordinate federal activities and work closely with state and local governments. There are some people who would insist that the Federal Government should stay out of the picture, but this is impossible, because there are certain aspects of the problem, certain critically distressed areas for example, that will require the kind of massive support that only the Federal Government can provide.

There is, however, the ever-present danger that, well-intentioned though they may be, remedies will cost more than the ill effects of the ailment they seek to cure. This is a continuing challenge to all of us who want to correct soundly and effectively a situation as serious as chronic unemployment.

Now let us look at the other responsibility of government, which exists not only at the federal but at the state and local levels: the job of dealing with the problem of chronic unemployment. It seems to me that these are the remedial steps that can be taken:

1] *An objective and thorough study* to determine the extent, location, and underlying cause of chronic unemployment.

2] *A greatly strengthened program of vocational training*, to train the untrained and to retrain those whose original skills are no longer needed.

3] *More effective career guidance for young people.*

4] *Better information about employment opportunities* in other portions of a given state, or elsewhere in the country.

5] *Industrial development programs* on a local and regional basis.

6] *Public education* on the evils of racial and age discrimination.

7] *Financial incentives to the individuals while under retraining.* (The obvious possibilities are permitting him to deduct the cost of his training from his income tax and giving him special unemployment-compensation benefits.)

In the final analysis, from the standpoint of the unemployed man or woman, *we are talking about the ability of people to do the job that is available to them.* Unfortunately, there are some people who feel that a man's ability to do a job is automatically determined by his race or his age. Racial discrimination or age discrimination is unjust and un-American. It also is economically wasteful because it deprives human beings of their right to play a full role in their country's economic well-being. Both of these problem areas require constant education and reeducation about the necessity for equal opportunity, and I am confident of the ultimate outcome, if for no other reason than the American public's sense of fair play.

It seems to me that an especially difficult problem is presented by the individual who becomes unemployed because he lacks the necessary skills or the necessary education to keep up with the changing job requirements of his industry. This problem could live to haunt him all the rest of his working life—provided he has a working life. Here is the challenge of training and retraining our displaced workers so that they can reenter the working force. Now, then, whose problem is this? As I pointed out a moment ago, it is an individual company's problem to train or retrain those who can be absorbed into that company's working force, but there are reasonable limits beyond which industry cannot be expected to go. There must be a reasonable indication that the individual is capable of absorbing the new training, and there must be a job available to him when he completes it. Carrying the training function beyond this point is the job of public education, and this is the point at which the local community enters into the picture.

Vocational high schools for young people are an established fact in countless communities, and so are hobby classes for adults, but I am talking about *full-range vocational courses for adults.* Certain communities will need far more ambitious programs than others, and it is conceivable that some communities will soon find themselves over their heads financially. Here would be the logical justification for state aid, or if the state itself were in an economic decline, for federal assistance, but the community should first be required to utilize every resource directly available to it to solve its own problems to the best of its abilities, and then turn to the government for such help as it legitimately needs.

There is another aspect of this problem that presents many difficulties, and that is exemplified by the young person who leaves school before he is adequately prepared for today's employment market, let alone for the far more complicated requirements of tomorrow. Here again is a grave challenge to the local community.

In recent years, greatly increased attention has been given to the need for higher education, with particularly great emphasis on the need for scientists and engineers. Thankfully, this concern has also been broadened to include all types of higher education, including the arts, business administration, the social sciences, and the professions. Certainly, this concern is commendable, but it has tended to divert attention away from an equally important area of education, which is the need for more effective career guidance for our high school students.

As someone who has been active in local school affairs for many years, I have been disturbed at the tendency of local school systems to give inadequate attention to vocational training and career guidance of young people. There is nothing more pathetic than the youngster leaving high school as soon as the legal attendance requirements are met, only to find himself just one of hundreds of thousands of unskilled, unneeded job applicants. This situation is compounded by the fact that this youngster may never make the grade, and may well be a frequently recurring unemployment statistic for the rest of his life. There are very few communities in the country that do not have this situation confronting them in some manner.

These recommendations about training and retraining all presuppose that the community either is strong enough to support the activity or can obtain state or federal aid. But it also presupposes that there are employment opportunities in that community. Unfortunately, this is frequently not the case, and we are therefore confronted with the necessity for breathing new economic life into some communities and, in fact, into entire regions.

Many communities have formed industrial-development committees to encourage new industries and to improve the business climate of the area. Our company's various operations throughout the country are very active in these organizations, and we feel that important progress is being made. Major expansion projects have been initiated and widespread public interest has been generated, with the result that the community is becoming a far better place in which to live—and to *work*. But a great deal remains to be done.

Regardless of the dislocations I have mentioned, the fact remains that, if this country is to attain the rate of economic growth that all of us know we must attain, we will soon find that our rate of automation will have to be increased if we are to meet the demands of the future. The demand for skilled and suitably educated workers will continue to rise in this country, and we will find it necessary to review very drastically some of our traditional concepts of education to meet this expanding need. Just as it is in the armed services, where constant training in the most modern of methods is necessary for survival, so will it be in the case of the civilian worker. Education in the years ahead will be a continuous, never-ending process, as the individual equips himself to deal with a constantly changing world.

I realize that I have covered many subjects in these pages, but this is a reflection of the complex nature of the challenges confronting the managers of American industry. Our steadily rising standard of living, the phenomenal growth in the quality and quantity of the goods and services we demand, and the increasing complexity of the economic machine required to produce these goods and services present all of us with an entirely new set of problems. However, as I pointed out at the very start, the challenges are far more than domestic, because we must also maintain our competitive position in the world market. This means that we must not only find new and better ways of doing things throughout our economic system, but the benefits of these advances must be apportioned equally to all of the major groups in our economy—the people who have invested their savings in our industries, the people who work in our industries, and the people who buy our products—in fact, to *everyone*. If any one of these groups demands preferential treatment over the others, the future of this country will be severely restricted. By the same token, unless industry and government make sure that they understand their respective roles in a free enterprise system, and unless they cooperate with each other in attaining their goals, we will miss the opportunities that lie ahead of us.

Needless to say, I am confident that these challenges will be met head on—with tenacity, imagination, and skill.

Closing an Obsolete Facility

THIS CASE HISTORY points out the inescapable fact that whereas the long-term benefits of automation are obvious to all of us, there is no denying that short-term dislocations can occur. The person who becomes unemployed knows only that he has lost his job; the long-term trend is no source of consolation to him. This places a great responsibility on management, a responsibility to plan carefully and thoroughly, to use every skill and resource to keep its facilities competitive and thus safeguard employment, but if dislocations cannot be avoided, to implement a well-devised program, extending over a reasonable period of time, to ease the impact of loss of employment.

Our Sylvania subsidiary, which produces a wide range of electronic and electrical products, would never have reached its present size, with all of the accompanying job opportunities, without large-scale use of automatic and semiautomatic manufacturing equipment. While the company's total employment has remained relatively constant in the past several years, the composition of that total has changed considerably. Manufacturing employment has decreased, whereas scientific, technical, sales, and administrative employment has increased. In fact, one of Sylvania's largest divisions, which has grown very rapidly in the past four or five years, has a total employment today of more than 7,000, of which about 40 percent are technical personnel. While the products of this division are highly complex electronic systems and equipment for the armed services, which do not lend themselves to automatic production methods, this example illustrates a trend in certain aspects of our operations.

On the other side of the coin, one of Sylvania's electronic-tube-manufacturing plants is gradually being "phased out," so to speak, because it is no longer competitive. This facility is the oldest of six receiving-tube plants, and we reluctantly came to the conclusion in the latter part of 1960 that it would be prohibitive from a cost standpoint to attempt to renovate the building and to install the newer types of machines so that costs would be in line with competition. This was compounded by the fact that the total demand for the types of electronic tube in question had leveled off due to the increasing use of transistors and other new devices in certain end products in which tubes had previously been used. Low-cost foreign competition was another important factor. At the same time, the productivity of a relatively new plant in another part of the state had been rising steadily, as the result of new and improved equipment and more advanced production methods, to the point that the newer plant could absorb the production requirements of the old plant.

This newer plant, incidentally, has played a major role in rehabilitating the economy of the community and surrounding area. This is illustrated, it seems to me, by the fact that the production machines are now serviced by men who formerly were employed as railroad car mechanics, but had been laid off when the local railroad shops curtailed their operations.

Now, then, what are we doing to assure that the closing of the other plant is accomplished with a minimum of hardship and dislocation? First of all, when we reached our decision to close the plant gradually over a period of six months, the plant manager called a meeting of all of the 500 employees and fully explained the circumstances to them. He had already alerted the state commerce department, the unemployment compensation department, and the state employment service.

A complete brochure was prepared, pointing out that while the plant was outmoded for electronics production, it could readily be adapted for other manufacturing or some other type of business.

The plant manager obtained a list of every employer of 100 or more people within a radius of 50 miles and wrote to each of them, explaining why the plant was being closed and highly recommending his employees. It goes without saying that he had also surveyed other Sylvania divisions, especially those in other communities in the state. In addition, he established an employment office in the plant as a point of contact for other companies.

Over the course of the six-month period ending July 1, attrition will take care of some of the problems, the annual attrition rate being about 30 percent (this stems from the fact that most of the plant's employees are women, and many of them are secondary wage-earners).

Now, then, what is the company doing to ease the dislocation? In addition to the job assistance program, the employees will be aided by a severance-pay plan. It is estimated that the average severance payment will exceed $800. (Cash payment equal to one day's straight-time pay for each of first five years of continuous service plus one week's straight-time pay for each year over five years.) An employee with 14 years of continuous service would receive 10 weeks straight-time pay, and an employee with 10 years of continuous service would receive six weeks straight-time pay.

Employees who are members of the company's savings and retirement plan will receive additional lump-sum payments based on their own and company contributions to the plan, plus accumulated interest on both.

We are very proud of a letter we received from the secretary of commerce of that state, who wrote: "Thankfully we don't have too many of these plant closings, but I seldom have seen one handled as well as you are handling this one, and Sylvania has reason to be proud of itself."

Administrative Automation

The Adoption of Centralized Data-Processing

IN 1954 we began a comprehensive study of the growing problem of providing adequate information to our decentralized plant and laboratory operations throughout the country. Aside from being a current problem, we could see the situation becoming aggravated by the steadily growing intensity of competition in the electronics business. This intensified competition was making it increasingly clear that the managers of our decentralized operations required more complete, more accurate, and more timely information upon which to base faster decisions. Our approach to the problem was to explore the advisability of automating our record-keeping and statistical work through the use of the electronic computer and its related equipment, all of which adds up to electronic data-processing.

It soon became apparent that we could no longer afford decentralized record-keeping using conventional methods, since these procedures would not provide adequate information at less than a prohibitive cost in clerical personnel. We also knew that we could not afford the high cost of using electronic computers on a decentralized basis. The net result was our decision to establish a nationwide data-processing network feeding a wide range of information into a data-processing center.

Once the decision was made, we embarked on an employee orientation program. We explained the problem we were attempting to solve, the reasons we had decided upon electronic data-processing as the answer, how long it would take to establish the new system, and how it would affect them personally. Having thus obtained employee understanding of the problem, we went to work programming the changeover, and over a period of three years the gradual transition was accomplished. Bearing in mind that the new system required the closing of record-keeping operations in various locations around the country, the changeover was accomplished in ample time to absorb the displaced employees in the new assignments or give the others sufficient time to relocate, although there were relatively few of the latter.